THE STATES AND THEIR SYMBOLS

Puerto Rico
Facts and Symbols

by Kathy Feeney

Consultant:
Ramón Bosque-Pérez, Researcher
Center for Puerto Rican Studies
Hunter College, City University of New York

Hilltop Books

an imprint of Capstone Press
Mankato, Minnesota

Hilltop Books are published by Capstone Press
151 Good Counsel Drive, P.O. Box 669, Mankato, Minnesota 56002
http://www.capstone-press.com

Library of Congress Cataloging-in-Publication Data
Feeney, Kathy, 1954–
    Puerto Rico facts and symbols/by Kathy Feeney.
    p. cm.—(The states and their symbols)
    Includes bibliographical references and index.
    Summary: Presents information about Puerto Rico, its nickname, motto,
and emblems.
    ISBN 0-7368-0644-X
    1. Emblems, National—Puerto Rico—Juvenile literature. [1. Emblems,
National—Puerto Rico. 2. Puerto Rico.] I. Title. II. Series.
CR341 .F44 2001
972.95—dc21   00-023946

Editorial Credits
Karen L. Daas, editor; Linda Clavel, production designer and illustrator;
    Kimberly Danger and Heidi Schoof, photo researchers

Photo Credits
James P. Rowan, 8, 22 (middle)
Leopoldo Miranda-Castro, 14
Mark Bacon, cover, 6, 12, 16, 18, 22 (top and bottom)
One Mile Up, Inc., 12 (inset)
Puerto Rico Tourism Company/Bob Krist, 20

2 3 4 5 6 06 05 04 03 02

Table of Contents

Atlantic Ocean

Arecibo Observatory

Old San Juan

San Juan

Bayamen ● ● Carolina

El Yunque
National Forest

PUERTO RICO

● Ponce

Caribbean Sea

★ Capital
○ Municipality
Places to
Visit

Fast Facts

Capital: San Juan is the capital of Puerto Rico.

Largest Municipality: San Juan is the largest municipality in Puerto Rico. About 439,400 people live there.

Size: The island of Puerto Rico covers 3,508 square miles (9,086 square kilometers).

Location: Puerto Rico lies southeast of the U.S. mainland.

Population: 3,860,091 people live in Puerto Rico (U.S. Census Bureau, 1999 estimate).

Commonwealth: In 1952, Puerto Rico became a commonwealth of the United States.

Natural Resources: Puerto Rico has copper, nickel, and stone.

Manufactured Goods: Puerto Rico's businesses produce appliances, electronics, computer equipment, medicine, plastic products, and rum.

Crops: Farmers in Puerto Rico grow bananas, coffee, pineapples, and sugar cane. They raise cattle and chickens. Crayfish and tuna are important Puerto Rican sea crops.

The Commonwealth

Puerto Rico is an island southeast of Florida. The Atlantic Ocean borders Puerto Rico on the north. The Caribbean Sea lies south of the island. The island's official name is the Commonwealth of Puerto Rico.

The island became part of the United States after the Spanish-American War (1898). The Spanish signed the Treaty of Paris to end this war. This agreement gave Puerto Rico, the Philippines, and Guam to the United States.

Puerto Rico became a U.S. commonwealth in 1952. Puerto Rico is not a state. But Puerto Rico is part of the United States. Puerto Ricans are American citizens. But Puerto Rico's citizens cannot vote in U.S. elections.

Some people believe Puerto Rico will become the 51st state. Others want it to remain a commonwealth. Still others hope that Puerto Rico will someday become an independent country.

The Atlantic Ocean and Caribbean Sea border Puerto Rico.

Puerto Rico's original name came from the people who first lived there. The Taínos called the island "Boriquén." This name means "the land of the valiant one."

Christopher Columbus visited the island in 1493. Columbus called it "San Juan." This name honors Saint John the Baptist.

Explorer Juan Ponce de Leon visited the island in 1508. In 1509, Ponce de Leon became the island's first governor. He renamed the island Puerto Rico. This Spanish name means "rich port." In 1952, the island's official name became the Commonwealth of Puerto Rico.

Puerto Rico's nickname is Isla del Encanto. This Spanish phrase means "Island of Enchantment." Puerto Rico is a popular vacation spot. The island's sandy beaches and tropical rain forests attract visitors from all around the world.

El Yunque is a tropical rain forest in Puerto Rico. Many people visit El Yunque each year.

JOANNES EST NOMEN EJUS

Seal and Motto

Puerto Rico's government adopted its seal in 1952. The seal represents Puerto Rico's government. The seal also makes commonwealth papers official.

Puerto Rico's seal is based on the coat of arms granted in 1511 by King Ferdinand and Queen Isabella of Spain. A lamb in the center of a green circle represents peace. The letters "F" and "I" are at the top of the green circle. These letters stand for Ferdinand and Isabella. Ferdinand and Isabella ruled Spain when Columbus discovered what is now Puerto Rico.

A border around the green circle shows Spanish symbols. Royal lions, towers, and flags represent Spain.

Puerto Rico's motto appears at the bottom of the seal. "Joannes Est Nomen Ejus" means "Juan is his name." Columbus originally named Puerto Rico "San Juan."

In 1511, Puerto Rico was a Spanish colony. The king and queen of Spain gave the colony a coat of arms at that time.

Capitol and Flag

San Juan is the capital of Puerto Rico. Puerto Rico's capitol building is in San Juan. Government officials meet there to make the commonwealth's laws.

Rafael Carmoega designed Puerto Rico's capitol. Workers built Puerto Rico's capitol in 1925. They built the capitol from Georgia marble.

Several mosaics are inside the capitol. Puerto Rican artists created these pictures. The mosaics show Puerto Rico's history.

A group of Puerto Ricans in New York City designed a flag for Puerto Rico in 1895. Puerto Rican officials had ordered this group to leave the island. Members of this group were fighting to make Puerto Rico an independent country.

Officials adopted the flag in 1952. The flag has red and white horizontal stripes. A blue triangle is on the left side of the flag. A five-pointed white star is centered on the blue triangle.

Architect Rafael Carmoega modeled Puerto Rico's capitol after the U.S. Capitol.

Commonwealth Bird

In 1980, Puerto Rico's government proposed adopting the reinita común as the island's official bird. The vote never passed. But people still consider the reinita the commonwealth bird.

Reinitas are songbirds. Their song sounds like a high-pitched whistle.

Reinitas build their nests in the mountains or gardens. Reinitas build two nests at the same time. One nest is used to lay eggs. The other nest is only for sleeping.

Male reinitas are black and yellow. Females are green, brown, and gray. Both male and female reinitas have a white stripe above their eyes and a white spot on each wing.

Reinitas grow to be 4 to 5 inches (10 to 13 centimeters) long. Reinitas have a long curved beak. They use their beak to eat bananas, insects, and flower nectar.

Several kinds of reinitas live throughout Puerto Rico. Reinita is Spanish for "little queen."

Commonwealth Tree

The Institute of Puerto Rican Culture suggested the ceiba as the commonwealth tree. The government has not officially adopted the symbol. But most people still consider the ceiba to be the commonwealth tree.

Ceibas grow in tropical climates. Their small yellow, white, or pink flowers bloom only at night. Bats pollinate the blossoms. Ceibas grow to be more than 100 feet (30 meters) tall. Their trunks stretch outward at the base. The trunk's shape keeps the huge trees planted firmly in moist soil.

Ceiba is a Caribbean Indian word that means canoe. Taínos used the ceiba's trunk to build canoes.

People also call ceibas kapok trees. The trees have seedpods filled with kapok. This soft, fluffy fiber is lightweight and waterproof. People stuff sleeping bags, life preservers, and pillows with kapok. Kapok also provides insulation from heat and sound.

Puerto Ricans consider ceibas a symbol of strength.

Commonwealth Flower

In 1980, Puerto Rican officials suggested the maga be named the commonwealth's official flower. But they never voted on the proposal. Most people still consider the maga to be a Puerto Rican symbol.

Maga flowers grow on maga trees. Maga trees grow in several of Puerto Rico's forests. These evergreen trees can grow to be 50 feet (15 meters) tall.

Magas are tropical trees that bloom all year. Magas have large red flowers with five bell-shaped petals. Maga flowers open in the morning and close at night. Most blooms last just one day.

Magas belong to the hibiscus family of flowers. People sometimes call the maga Puerto Rican hibiscus or flor de maga. People may eat maga blooms. They make dyes from the flowers. Some Puerto Rican women wear maga flowers in their hair.

Magas have large red flowers with five bell-shaped petals.

Commonwealth Animal

The coquí is Puerto Rico's unofficial animal. This tiny tree frog is very popular throughout the island. Puerto Ricans put its picture on everything from shirts to billboards.

The coquí is named for the sound it makes at night. Its call sounds like "co-kee." Visitors often mistake the frog's sound for a songbird.

Coquís are nocturnal. They sleep during the day and are active at night. They prefer dark moist places. Coquís sing from sunset to sunrise.

Coquís eat insects. They hunt for food on the ground and in trees.

Unlike other frogs, the coquí does not have webbed feet. It has separate toes. Pads on its toes keep the coquí from slipping on smooth surfaces.

Coquís change color to blend with their surroundings. Their color ranges from light green to dark brown.

Sixteen kinds of coquís live in Puerto Rico.

Places to Visit

Arecibo Observatory

The Arecibo Observatory is near the town of Arecibo. This observatory has the world's largest radar-radio telescopic dish. Scientists use this giant aluminum dish to study the universe. Visitors see the giant telescope from the center's observation platform.

El Yunque, Caribbean National Forest

El Yunque is near San Juan. Scientists conduct research in this tropical forest. Many animal species live in El Yunque. They include the Puerto Rican giant green lizard, the Puerto Rican parrot, and the Puerto Rican boa. Visitors hike through the rain forest and swim under waterfalls.

Old San Juan

Old San Juan is the "historical heart" of the city of San Juan. Old San Juan has narrow stone streets with outdoor cafes and colorful buildings from the 1500s. Visitors tour forts such as El Morro and Castillo de San Cristobal. They also visit La Fortaleza, the home of Puerto Rico's governor.

Words to Know

commonwealth (KOM-uhn-welth)—a region that is governed by the people who live there

explorer (ek-SPLOR-ur)—a person who travels to a new place to discover what it is like

insulation (in-suh-LAY-shun)—a material that stops heat, sound, or cold from entering or escaping

municipality (myoo-niss-uh-PAL-uh-tee)—a town or city

observatory (uhb-ZUR-vuh-tor-ee)—a building with telescopes and other scientific instruments for studying the sky, stars, and planets

pollinate (POL-uh-nate)—to carry pollen that is used to fertilize plants to produce a seed

valiant (VAL-yuhnt)—brave or courageous

Read More

Fradin, Dennis B. *Puerto Rico.* From Sea to Shining Sea. Danbury, Conn.: Children's Press, 1998.

Kummer, Patricia K. *Puerto Rico.* One Nation. Mankato, Minn: Capstone Books, 1999.

Landau, Elaine. *Puerto Rico.* A True Book. New York: Children's Press, 1999.

Useful Addresses

**Puerto Rico Convention &
Visitors Bureau**
255 Recinto Sur
San Juan, PR 00901

**Puerto Rico Tourism
Company**
666 Fifth Avenue
New York, NY 10103-1599

Internet Sites

Arecibo Observatory
http://www.naic.edu
Commonweatlh of Puerto Rico
http://www.50states.com/puerto.htm
State and Local Government on the Net—Puerto Rico
http://www.statelocalgov.net/pr.htm
Welcome to Puerto Rico
http://Welcome.toPuertoRico.org

Index